# What happens
## when you
# TALK?

Published by Evans Brothers Limited
2A Portman Mansions
Chiltern Street
London W1M 1LE

First published in Great Britain in 1984 by
Hamish Hamilton Children's Books

Reprinted 1985, 1987
New edition published 1992

The author and publishers would like to thank Dr R. H.
James MB, BS, FFARCS for his help and advice with the
preparation of this book.

Printed in Hong Kong and bound in China

ISBN 0 237 60201 6

# What happens when you TALK?

Joy Richardson

Illustrated by
Colin and Moira Maclean

Evans

Evans Brothers Limited

Your voice started working
as soon as you were born.
You used it for crying.

Sometimes you cried softly.
Sometimes you cried loudly.
But you could not talk.

You listened to people talking.
Soon you tried making sounds
with your mouth —
bababa
gagaga
dadada
It was fun making sounds.

Slowly you learned to fit
sounds together.
The sounds made words.
The words had meanings.
You talked and people understood you.

Your brain is in charge of talking.
It sends orders to your
voice-box and your mouth.

Put your hand round the front
of your neck.
Look in a mirror and say
'What happens when you talk?

Can you feel your voice-box working?
Can you see your mouth moving?

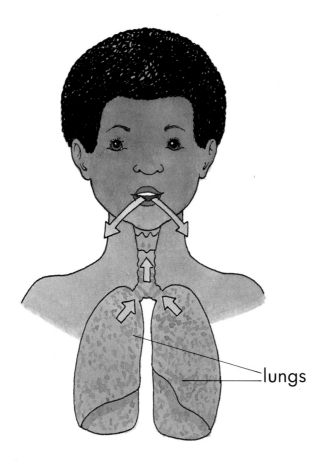

lungs

When you breathe out,
the air from your lungs
comes up your windpipe.
It goes through your voice-box
and out of your mouth.
You can use the air for talking.

Hold your breath and say your name.

Breathe out and say your name.

Breathe in and say your name.

Which is the best way of talking?

You cannot talk when you are
holding your breath.
Talking sounds funny when
you are breathing in.
You can only talk properly
when you are breathing out.

Your voice-box is at the
top of your windpipe.
It has a slit in the middle,
like a letter-box.

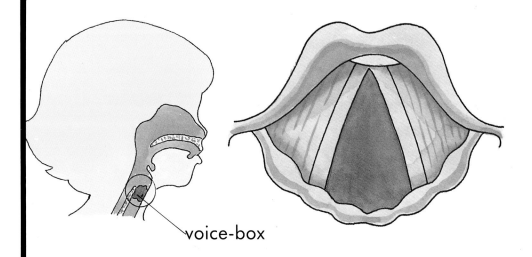

voice-box

When you are not talking,
the slit is wide open.
The air goes through
without making a noise.

On each side of the slit
there is a flap.
The flaps are your vocal cords.
They are like strong rubber bands
inside a special skin.

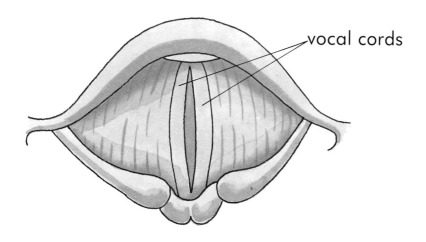

vocal cords

When you talk,
the vocal cords tighten up.
They make the slit narrower.

vocal cords
vibrating

Air pushes through the narrow slit.
It pushes against your vocal cords
and makes them vibrate.
They shake up and down very fast
and make a noise.

Put an elastic band
round an empty plastic tub.
Flick the elastic band
with your finger.
What do you see and hear?

The elastic band vibrates very fast.
As it vibrates, it makes a noise.

The air pushes against your vocal cords.
It makes them vibrate like this.

Blow a little air into a balloon.
Hold the neck between your finger
and thumb.
Let the air rush out.

Blow a lot of air into the balloon
and try again.
What do you see and hear?

The air made the neck
of the balloon vibrate.
A little air made a little noise.
A lot of air made a lot of noise.

When you talk loudly, a lot of air
pushes against your vocal cords.

With one breath, how many times
can you shout your name?
How many times can you say
your name quietly?
Loud talking uses up more air
than quiet talking.

Sing a song.
Listen to the high sounds
and low sounds
your voice can make.

Muscles in your voice-box
make your vocal cords
tighter for high sounds and
looser for low sounds.

Use a plastic tub again,
with an elastic band round it.
Pull the band out from one side
and hook it over a door handle.
Pull the tub away so that
the band over the top gets tighter.
Flick the elastic band as you
pull it tighter and tighter.

Can you hear the sound getting
higher as the elastic band
gets tighter **?**

Your mouth catches the sound
from your voice-box.
It turns it into the sounds
of letters and words.

Look at your face in a mirror.
Say a nursery rhyme slowly.
What can you see moving?

When you talk, your lips
open and close.
Your jaw goes up and down.
Your tongue moves about.

Your mouth has to make a
different shape for each sound.

When you change the shape
of your lips, the sound changes too.

Look in a mirror and say
a  e  i  o  u –

Squash up your lips and say oooo

Stretch them out and say eeee.

Sometimes you close your lips
and then let the sound burst out.
Put your hand in front of
your mouth and say —
    p   b

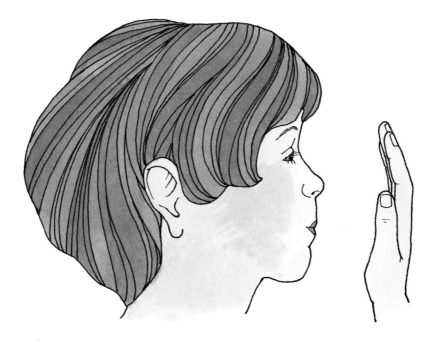

Can you feel the air rushing out?

Work out where your tongue goes
when you say –
    c   d   s

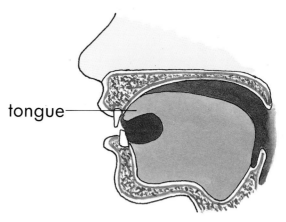

tongue

Work out where your teeth go
when you say –
    f  r

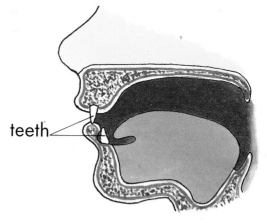

teeth

Your mouth has to change shape
quickly to get ready for
the next sound.

Can you say these tongue-twisters
five times quickly without
getting your mouth into a muddle?

Run one run son!

Six mixed biscuits.

The clean queen's clown.

Men have longer vocal cords
than women and children.
So their voices sound deeper.
When boys are about thirteen,
their voices get deeper too.

The spaces inside our mouths and
noses and throats are different shapes.
So our voices all sound different.

Use elastic bands to fix
pieces of paper over the tops
of four containers (such as
a mug, a tub, a bottle and a bowl).
Tap each paper top with your finger.
Can you hear how differently-shaped
containers change the sound?

Close your eyes.
Ask everyone in the room
to say your name, one at a time.
How many different voices
can you recognise?

# INDEX